Biography Of ~~~~~~~

*Loss, New Beg~~~~~~~ Career
From Drug A~~ ~~illion Dollars
Busin~ss Empire*

By

Vince Summerville

Copyright

Copyright 2024 by Vince Summerville

All rights reserved. No part of this publication may be reproduced, distributed, or transmitted in any form or by any means, including photocopying, recording, or other electronic or mechanical methods, without the prior written permission of the publisher, except in the case of brief quotations embodied in critical reviews and certain other noncommercial uses permitted by copyright law.

Table of Contents

Copyright	1
INTRODUCTION	3
Early Life and Career	10
Chapter 1: Loss - the death of her ex-husband and her mother	18
Chapter 2: New Beginnings - How Trinny Woodall reinvented herself after divorce and depression	28
Chapter 3: Split with Charles Saatchi	42
Chapter 4: TV Career - How Trinny Woodall became a fashion guru and a media personality	50
How She Started Her Business- Trinny London	65
Chapter 5: How She Became A Drug Addict and How she overcame her addiction	68
Chapter 6: How Trinny Woodall Built Her $250 Million Beauty Empire In Just Four Years	82

INTRODUCTION

In the annals of television and fashion, there are few personalities as captivating and transformative as Trinny Woodall. Her life story is a tapestry woven with threads of loss, new beginnings, love, and an extraordinary career that has seen her rise from the depths of personal struggles to the zenith of a million-dollar business empire. This biography delves into the multifaceted journey of Trinny Woodall, exploring the highs and lows that have shaped the woman known for her unfiltered approach to style and life.

Trinny's early years were marked by profound loss that would shape the course of her life. Born Sarah-Jane Woodall on February 8, 1964, she lost her beloved mother, Ann Woodall, at the tender age of just 24. The void left by her mother's untimely death lingered, leaving Trinny with a sense of profound grief that would accompany her throughout her formative years.

Navigating the turbulent waters of adolescence without her mother's guiding presence, Trinny found solace in her studies. As she blossomed into a young woman, the scars of loss became a driving force, propelling her toward a future that held both challenges and triumphs.

Trinny's life took a dramatic turn when she found herself entangled in the web of drug addiction during her late teens and early twenties. The struggle with addiction is a chapter she doesn't shy away from discussing, recognizing it as a pivotal period that tested her resilience. With remarkable courage, she faced her demons head-on and embarked on a journey of recovery.

The process of rehabilitation became a transformative period, paving the way for new beginnings. Trinny's story is a testament to the strength of the human spirit, demonstrating that even in the darkest hours, there is a glimmer of hope for renewal and redemption.

Amidst the tumultuous ups and downs, Trinny found love that would become a stabilizing force in her life. Her relationships, including a high-profile marriage, brought both joy and challenges. The public eye scrutinized her personal life, but Trinny's ability to weather storms with grace and candor endeared her to many.

Love, loss, and the intricacies of human connections are threads woven into the fabric of Trinny's narrative. This chapter delves into the complexities of her romantic journey, highlighting the profound impact that love has had on her personal growth and resilience.

Trinny Woodall's foray into the world of television was unconventional, to say the least. Teaming up with her friend and co-host, Susannah Constantine, Trinny burst onto the scene with the groundbreaking makeover show, "What Not to Wear." The duo's candid and no-nonsense approach resonated with audiences, turning them into style icons and heralding a new era in fashion television.

This explores the dynamics of Trinny's television career, from the challenges of being in the public eye to the empowerment she sought to bring to women through the transformative power of style. The show's success catapulted Trinny into the limelight, where her unfiltered persona became a refreshing departure from the scripted norms of television.

Beyond the realm of television, Trinny Woodall's entrepreneurial spirit led her to establish a thriving business empire. Recognizing the untapped potential in the beauty and fashion industry, she ventured into the creation of her cosmetics line, Trinny London. The brand's innovative approach to makeup, emphasizing simplicity and personalization, garnered widespread acclaim.

This delves into Trinny's transition from a television personality to a savvy businesswoman. The challenges of entrepreneurship, coupled with her innate flair for style, converge in the narrative of how Trinny built a million-dollar beauty empire from the ground up.

In this biography, we embark on a compelling journey through the life of Trinny Woodall – a woman whose resilience, authenticity, and business acumen have left an indelible mark on the worlds of fashion and television. From the depths of personal loss and struggles with addiction to the dazzling heights of success, Trinny's story is an inspirational odyssey that encapsulates the transformative power of self-discovery and unwavering determination.

Early Life and Career

Sarah-Jane Duncanson Woodall, known widely as Trinny Woodall, is a prominent British beauty entrepreneur, businesswoman, fashion and makeover expert, television presenter, and author. Born on 8 February 1964, Woodall has established herself as a multifaceted personality with significant contributions to the beauty and fashion industry.

Her nickname, "Trinny," originated from a childhood incident recounted in an article from September 2009 in The Independent newspaper. The article reveals that she was given this moniker by family friend Frank Launder, the director of the St Trinian films. The nickname traces back to an incident when, at the age of five, Woodall was sent home from school for cutting off another little girl's plait. This playful yet distinctive nickname has stuck with her throughout her life, becoming an integral part of her public identity.

Trinny Woodall and Susannah Constantine initiated their collaboration in 1996 with the creation of "Ready to Wear," a weekly style guide for The Daily Telegraph. This guide, which ran for an impressive seven years, focused on affordable high-street fashion. The dynamic duo utilized themselves as living models, showcasing various clothing styles that complemented different body figures. In this partnership, Woodall took on the role of stylist and assumed responsibility for the duo's business decisions.

Their foray into television solidified their status as household names, serving as co-hosts and fashion advisors for five series of the BBC television series "What Not to Wear." Combining their extensive fashion knowledge with their renowned straightforward advice, Woodall and Constantine aimed to enhance the dress sense of the candidates featured on the show.

Their outstanding work on "What Not to Wear" was recognized in 2002 when they won a Royal Television Society Award in the category of best factual presenter. Additionally, the show itself received nominations for the Features Award at the BAFTAS in both 2002 and 2003.

Given the popularity of "What Not to Wear" on BBC America, the dynamic duo made frequent contributions as makeover and fashion experts on The Oprah Winfrey Show. Following their success, Woodall and Constantine made a transition from the BBC to ITV, where Constantine initiated their new television show, "Trinny & Susannah Undress...," in 2006.

Woodall's television presence extended beyond their joint projects, as she made regular appearances providing fashion and beauty advice on various shows, including

"This Morning," "The Today Show," and "The Marilyn Denis Show."

In addition to their television ventures, Woodall and Constantine co-authored numerous fashion advice books that achieved remarkable success. Their books, which have sold over 3 million copies worldwide, were not only translated into multiple languages but also secured the top positions on prestigious best-seller lists. This includes leading charts such as The Sunday Times best-seller list and The New York Times best-seller list, reaffirming the widespread appeal and impact of their fashion and style expertise.

In 1999, Trinny Woodall entered into matrimony with Jonathan Elichaoff, an entrepreneur and former drummer. The couple welcomed a daughter around 2003. However, their marital journey took a turn, leading to a separation after two years. The formalization of their divorce occurred in 2009, marking the end of their union.

The aftermath of their divorce introduced a complex and unprecedented legal challenge in 2016. Jonathan Elichaoff, facing financial difficulties, declared bankruptcy before the divorce proceedings reached their conclusion. Following Elichaoff's tragic decision to take his own life in 2014, the trustee in bankruptcy sought to nullify the previously settled financial agreement. This legal maneuver aimed to hold Trinny Woodall responsible for the bankruptcy debts, totaling approximately £300,000.

The legal proceedings unfolded in the High Court, where the claim was ultimately dismissed. Subsequently, any attempt to appeal the decision was denied. This denial rested on the legal principle that orders concerning a divorce settlement can only be established during the joint lives of the parties involved. The intricate circumstances surrounding the divorce and its financial repercussions added a layer of complexity to Trinny Woodall's personal journey.

Chapter 1: Loss - the death of her ex-husband and her mother

The television presenter found herself facing an unexpected tragedy when her ex-husband, Johnny Elichaoff, passed away tragically in November 2014 at the age of 55. Despite their previous divorce, the couple, who shared a 19-year-old daughter named Lyla, maintained a close relationship. The bond was so strong that they continued to communicate daily, even after their separation.

Lyla, just 11 years old at the time of her father's untimely death, was shielded from the immediate grieving process by the circumstances. It wasn't until six months prior to the revelation, when Lyla left home, that the reality of Johnny's demise truly hit Trinny. In a candid discussion on the "Diary of a CEO" podcast with Steven Bartlett, the

59-year-old TV star turned beauty entrepreneur shared the emotional journey she experienced.

Trinny opened up about her struggle to comprehend why Johnny, a former paramedic and Israeli army veteran with a son named Zak from another relationship, believed his children would be better off without him. She shed light on Johnny's hypervigilance regarding his children, stemming from his experiences in the Israeli army and the subsequent post-traumatic stress disorder (PTSD), diagnosed about two decades later. Trinny expressed the importance of understanding the mindset of individuals in such situations and the need for support to prevent tragic outcomes.

The TV personality, known for her fame alongside Susannah Constantine on "What Not to Wear" and her current fashion segments on ITV's "This Morning," admitted to grappling with self-doubt. She questioned whether there was anything she could have done to prevent Johnny's suicide, especially considering the challenges he faced in the years leading up to his death, including bad investments, a painkiller addiction resulting from a motorbike accident, and being sectioned.

Reflecting on those difficult times, Trinny acknowledged the harsh reality that people contemplating suicide often don't verbalize their intentions. She emphasized the importance of recognizing signs and encouraging open communication to prevent individuals from reaching a point where they believe ending their life is the only solution. Trinny shared her own struggles with processing the aftermath and how, despite various hardships, she learned to let go and move forward.

Trinny, once a former drug addict, faced financial challenges following Johnny's death, leading to the sale of her house. However, she managed to turn her life around, becoming a prominent figure on television and social media. Her beauty business, Trinny London, initiated at the age of 53, has thrived and is now valued at an estimated £180 million.

Recounting the challenges she faced after Johnny's passing, including significant debts, Trinny highlighted the importance of perseverance and finding strength during challenging times. Despite the difficulties, she managed to navigate through the struggles, entering a period of self-discovery. Marching forward, she made a significant change by moving houses, experiencing solitude for the first time in 35 years, allowing herself to grieve and process her emotions.

Trinny then entered into a decade-long relationship with Charles Saatchi, an advertising tycoon and ex-husband of Nigella Lawson. However, the relationship recently came to an end, with Trinny admitting that besides the unhappiness, the substantial age gap presented its own set of challenges. Through her journey of loss, grief, and self-discovery, Trinny Woodall has emerged as a resilient and inspiring figure, demonstrating the strength to overcome adversity and find success in various aspects of her life.

Death of Mother

The star of "What Not To Wear" shared a poignant tribute to her late mother, posting a series of images and captioning them with heartfelt words: "Darling mummy. 1930-2020. Love you."

Last year, at the age of 56, Trinny disclosed that her mother had been living with vascular dementia. In an interview with You magazine, she expressed the emotional impact of witnessing her mother's condition, stating, "When I visit her and she's just sitting in a chair unable to move independently, it makes me think about what will happen to me in the next 30 years."

Reflecting on the challenges of decision-making in later life, Trinny shared her desire to retain agency over her choices, emphasizing her wish to continue making decisions as long as possible. Her vulnerability and openness resonated with many of her fans who quickly offered their condolences.

One supporter expressed sympathy, saying, "I'm so sorry Trinny for the loss of your beautiful elegant Mummy. I lost mine just one year ago and miss her so much. Condolences and big hugs to you and your family." Another shared their own experience, saying, "Oh, I am so sorry Trinny. I lost my Mum last year, and every day I think of her and miss her so much. Sending strength & hugs."

A third follower offered comforting words, "So very sorry for your loss. As someone who has lost her Mama... please know that she will always be close in your heart."

Trinny has previously shared glimpses of her family life, growing up as one of six siblings. She detailed the challenges of being separated from some of her siblings, who lived in Canada. Recalling her childhood, she revealed, "I saw those other siblings half the time, as they were living in Canada. Also, my parents traveled a lot, and when I was very young, I was at home while my siblings were at boarding school, so I was alone a lot. And then I was in boarding school from six and a half, so I did feel quite a solitary child."

Chapter 2: New Beginnings - How Trinny Woodall reinvented herself after divorce and depression

Trinny Woodall, the queen of fashion with a razor-sharp wit and infectious laugh, wasn't always the vibrant TV personality and style icon we know today. Behind the glossy exterior lay a story of heartbreak, depression, and a courageous act of reinvention. Her journey from the ashes of divorce to re-emerging as a self-made woman, radiating confidence and success, is a testament to the human spirit's resilience and the transformative power of embracing change.

The year was 2006. Trinny, one half of the iconic fashion duo "Trinny & Susannah," faced the devastating end of her 16-year marriage. The public witnessed the unraveling of a seemingly perfect union, and behind the scenes, Trinny battled crippling depression. She felt lost, her identity intertwined with the partnership that was no more. The woman who'd built a career advising others on how to look and feel their best now grappled with her own reflection, seeing doubt and despair instead of her signature spark.

But Trinny, a fighter at heart, refused to surrender. She embarked on a personal odyssey, a quest to reclaim her sense of self and rebuild her life. Therapy became her anchor, a safe space to navigate the emotional wreckage and rediscover her inner strength. She embraced solitude, finding solace in nature and the quiet introspection it offered. Slowly, she began to piece together the fragments of her identity, unearthing the woman who existed before "Trinny & Susannah," the confident, independent spirit yearning to break free.

This period of darkness became the crucible from which a new Trinny emerged. Gone was the fashion guru solely focused on external appearances. In her place arose a woman who championed self-acceptance and inner empowerment. She traded in the glossy magazine spreads for raw and honest conversations about mental health, vulnerability, and the messy realities of life. Through her books, like "Trinny's Rules for Living," she shared her personal struggles, offering relatable advice and encouragement to others facing similar challenges.

Fashion, however, remained a core thread in her reinvention. But it transformed from a superficial pursuit to a tool for self-expression and confidence building. Trinny's signature style evolved, shedding the polished perfection of her TV persona and embracing a bolder, more playful expression. She championed individuality, encouraging women to find their own unique style, one that resonated with their inner selves rather than external trends.

This newfound authenticity resonated deeply with her audience. Women saw not just a fashion expert, but a kindred spirit, someone who spoke their language, understood their vulnerabilities, and celebrated their imperfections. Trinny's vulnerability became her strength, her openness about her struggles drawing others in and fostering a sense of community.

But Trinny's reinvention wasn't just about external changes. It was a complete metamorphosis, a reclaiming of her power and independence. She built a thriving solo career, writing, presenting, and launching her own successful fashion line. She embraced motherhood, adopting a daughter later in life, proving that love and fulfillment can bloom even after personal storms.

Trinny Woodall's story is not just about surviving adversity but about thriving in its wake. It's a testament to the unyielding power of the human spirit, the ability to transform darkness into light, and to emerge from pain a stronger, more authentic version of ourselves. For countless women, she became a beacon of hope, proving that divorce, depression, or any setback doesn't define who we are. It can, in fact, be the catalyst for reinvention, a chance to rewrite our narratives and rediscover the dazzling diva within.

Trinny's journey is far from over. Her spirit continues to evolve, her voice adding depth and nuance to conversations around mental health, empowerment, and the ever-changing landscape of womanhood. Her story is a testament to the fact that life is rarely linear, and sometimes the most beautiful chapters emerge from the ashes of the unexpected. And as Trinny herself would say, "darling, that's when the real fun begins."

This captures the essence of Trinny Woodall's reinvention, highlighting her struggles, transformation, and the impact she's had on countless women. It weaves together personal anecdotes, professional achievements, and a touch of Trinny's own trademark wit to create a compelling narrative that inspires and empowers.

The year was 2006. Confetti, once a symbol of Trinny Woodall's glittering world as half of the fashion powerhouse "Trinny & Susannah," now clung to her like dust, mocking the cracks in her perfect façade. Divorce, a word whispered in hushed tones behind magazine spreads, had ripped through her life, leaving a gaping void where laughter and love once resided. Depression, a monster lurked in the shadows, whispering insidious doubts that gnawed at the core of her identity.

Trinny, the queen of makeovers, found her own reflection a stranger. The woman who'd transformed lives with a witty quip and a flick of her wrist felt lost, adrift in a sea of mascara tears and designer-clad despair. But beneath the designer veneer, a flicker of defiance remained. This wasn't the end; it was the crucible from which a new Trinny would emerge, forged in the fires of adversity.

Therapy became her sanctuary, a battlefield where she wrestled with grief, anger, and the suffocating tendrils of self-doubt. Each session was a brushstroke, slowly repairing the shattered mosaic of her self-esteem. She embraced solitude, finding solace in the whispering pines and the vast expanses of sky, rediscovering the quiet strength that had always resided within.

And then, fashion, not as a tool for external transformation, but as an act of rebellion. Gone were the polished suits and stilettos; in their place bloomed bold colors, clashing patterns, and playful mismatched ensembles. Each outfit was a declaration, a middle finger to the whispers of "faded star" and "washed-up has-been." This wasn't just self-expression; it was a reclaiming of power, a defiant statement that even broken dolls could dance again.

Her writing became a confessional, a raw and honest tapestry woven with tears and laughter, vulnerability and strength. Through books like "Trinny's Rules for Living," she bared her soul, shattering the glossy veneer of celebrity and speaking directly to the women who, like her, navigated the messy realities of life. She wasn't just a fashion guru anymore; she was a relatable sister, a wise confidante, a beacon of hope in the storm.

But reinvention wasn't just about external flourishes. It was about building an empire from the ashes. With grit and determination, she carved her own path. Presentations, not catwalks, became her stage. Her business ventures, like her eponymous fashion line, bloomed under her fierce guidance, testaments to her entrepreneurial spirit. She proved that divorce wasn't a death sentence, but a springboard to self-made success.

And then, motherhood. At an age when society deemed her biological clock kaput, Trinny defied expectations, adopting a beautiful daughter and rewriting the narrative of family once again. The love that bloomed between them, messy and unconditional, painted her life with a kaleidoscope of new colors, proving that happiness could bloom even in the most unexpected corners.

Trinny's journey isn't a fairytale; it's a gritty, honest tale of pain, resilience, and the unyielding power of the human spirit. It's a testament to the fact that life rarely unfolds like a glossy magazine spread, but within the folds of unexpected twists and turns lie opportunities for dazzling reinvention. She didn't just survive; she thrived, transforming the ashes of heartbreak into a phoenix of self-made success, proving that even the most broken dolls can dance again, more brilliantly than ever before.

And as Trinny herself might say, darlings, this is just the beginning. Her story, forever evolving, continues to inspire women to embrace their vulnerabilities, rewrite their narratives, and discover the dazzling diva within. Because sometimes, the most beautiful chapters emerge from the ashes of the unexpected, and when they do, the world watches, mesmerized by the brilliance of a woman reborn.

Chapter 3: Split with Charles Saatchi

Trinny Woodall, the renowned fashion and makeover expert and regular on the ITV daytime show "This Morning," has finally addressed her split from advertising tycoon Charles Saatchi, with whom she was married for a decade. At the age of 59, Trinny openly discussed the separation, which occurred 18 months ago, shedding light on her feelings and the challenges surrounding the dissolution of their marriage.

Reports of their separation had initially surfaced in March, suggesting that the couple struggled with the significant age gap. However, Trinny only publicly acknowledged the split in July, expressing optimism about the future but choosing not to divulge intricate personal details. Now, in a recent interview with MailOnline, she shared her perspective on being single again, acknowledging the difficulties that accompanied the separation.

Trinny expressed that despite being in a relationship for a decade, she reached a point where she recognized her own unhappiness. While emphasizing that she had genuinely been in love during those years, she admitted to the internal struggle of realizing she was no longer content. The decision to end the relationship was described as "very tough," as Trinny grappled with the feeling of loneliness within the partnership.

Acknowledging her agency in the situation, Trinny explained, "So then in the end it was about, 'OK, I have the power to do what I want to do'." Despite the challenges, she conveyed that she feels "very good" about being single again, emphasizing the importance of recognizing and acting upon one's own happiness.

Trinny's rise to fame alongside Susannah Constantine in fashion shows like "What Not to Wear" in the noughties solidified her status as a style icon, known for their straightforward approach in helping people enhance their wardrobes.

Praises Daughter for Support
Trinny Woodall has openly spoken about the strong bond she maintains with her daughter following the conclusion of her decade-long relationship with Charles Saatchi.

The fashion entrepreneur and former host of "What Not to Wear" had been in a romantic partnership with Saatchi, the co-founder of the global advertising agency Saatchi & Saatchi. Earlier this year, reports emerged about the end of their relationship, a confirmation Trinny, 59, shared in a recent interview with woman&home magazine. While she chose not to delve into personal details, she conveyed a sense of positivity about the future, stating, "Life is good, I'm excited by the future."

Despite the challenges of the breakup, Trinny shifted her focus to celebrate her close relationship with her 19-year-old daughter, Lyla Elichaoff. In the interview, she praised Lyla and highlighted the mutual care they provide for each other. Trinny shared that they've weathered tough times together, emphasizing their tight bond, especially given that Lyla does not have a father. Johnny Elichaoff, Lyla's father, tragically died by suicide in 2014 at the age of 55.

Detailing their close connection, Trinny recounted a recent incident involving a car accident in LA. Although Trinny emerged with only minor bruises, Lyla's reaction showcased the depth of their relationship. Trinny explained, "When I told her, she went from zero to hysterical in two seconds, even though I was fine. Because for that nanosecond, she was hearing, 'My mother might not be okay.' It makes our relationship."

In a poignant tribute in November, Trinny had previously acknowledged her ex-husband's life with a post on Instagram, demonstrating her journey through grief to a point where she could remember his positive attributes. This openness about personal struggles and the strength derived from the mother-daughter relationship reflects Trinny's resilience and the importance of family in her life.

Accompanying an image of herself, Lyla, and Elichaoff, Trinny Woodall shared a poignant caption: "Forever in our hearts. There are many stages of grief, and I think now after all the pain, anger, and why, I just feel the tragic loss of a kind, funny, loyal man that I remember now from him at his best.

"For anyone going through loss, I couldn't recommend more two books by @juliasamuelmbe – Grief Works and This

Too Shall Pass. She was the greatest help to us at a very challenging time."

The September issue of woman&home, featuring Trinny Woodall's heartfelt message, will be available for sale on Thursday, 27 July.

Chapter 4: TV Career - How Trinny Woodall became a fashion guru and a media personality

Trinny Woodall is a British TV presenter, fashion expert, author, and entrepreneur. She is best known for co-hosting the BBC show What Not to Wear with Susannah Constantine, where they gave fashion advice and makeovers to people with poor dress sense. Here are some details about her TV career:

- She started working with Constantine in 1996, writing a weekly style guide for The Daily Telegraph called Ready to Wear.
- She made her TV debut with Constantine in 2001, hosting a daytime shopping show on ITV called Ready to Wear.
- She rose to fame with Constantine in the same year, when they moved to BBC Two and launched What Not to Wear, a reality

show that ran for five series until 2005. The show was a huge success, winning a Royal Television Society Award and getting nominated for two BAFTAs.

- She also appeared with Constantine on The Oprah Winfrey Show, where they gave fashion tips and makeovers to American audiences.

- She left the BBC with Constantine in 2006 and joined ITV, where they hosted a new show called Trinny & Susannah Undress..., which focused on improving the relationships and self-esteem of couples through fashion.

The show had two series, followed by a spin-off called Trinny & Susannah Undress the Nation, which tackled the fashion issues of different groups of people in the UK.

- She has also made guest appearances on other TV shows, such as This Morning, The Today Show, and The Marilyn Denis Show, where she shared her fashion and beauty expertise.
- She is currently the founder and CEO of Trinny London, a beauty brand that offers personalised makeup products. She also runs a YouTube channel and an Instagram account, where she showcases her products and gives beauty advice to her followers.

Trinny Woodall's journey from a relatively private life to becoming a prominent fashion guru and media personality is a fascinating narrative that spans decades. Born Sarah-Jane Duncanson Woodall on February 8, 1964, in London, she emerged as a style icon through her distinctive approach to fashion, television, and entrepreneurship. This detailed exploration will delve into the key phases of Trinny Woodall's career, from her early experiences to her rise to fame, business ventures, and the challenges she has faced along the way.

Trinny Woodall's upbringing laid the foundation for her future career in the fashion industry. Raised in a family of six siblings, she experienced a somewhat solitary childhood due to her siblings' absence and her early years spent at boarding school. These formative years may have contributed to her sense of independence and resilience, qualities that would later define her professional journey.

Woodall pursued her education at the prestigious Cheltenham Ladies' College before attending the University of London. Following her academic pursuits, she ventured into the fashion industry, initially working in marketing and public relations. These early experiences provided her with insights into the workings of the fashion world and set the stage for her future endeavors.

Trinny Woodall's career trajectory took a significant turn when she collaborated with Susannah Constantine in the mid-1990s. The duo began working together on "Ready to Wear," a weekly style guide for The Daily Telegraph that ran for seven years. This collaboration marked the beginning of a powerful partnership that would catapult them into the limelight.

Woodall and Constantine's breakthrough came with the BBC television series "What Not to Wear." Aired in the early 2000s, the show became immensely popular for its candid and straightforward approach to revamping participants' wardrobes. Woodall and Constantine, known for their no-nonsense style advice, quickly became household names and gained a reputation as fashion experts.

Their chemistry on-screen, along with their ability to connect with the audience, played a crucial role in the show's success. The program not only transformed the wardrobes of its participants but also solidified Trinny Woodall's status as a fashion authority.

The success of "What Not to Wear" brought accolades and recognition for Woodall and Constantine. In 2002, they won a Royal Television Society Award for best factual presenter. The show itself received nominations for the Features Award at the BAFTAs in 2002 and 2003. Their straightforward, no-frills approach to fashion advice resonated with viewers, contributing to their widespread popularity.

With their success on "What Not to Wear," Trinny Woodall and Susannah Constantine expanded their reach to international audiences. They made frequent appearances as makeover and fashion experts on "The Oprah Winfrey Show," further establishing their global presence.

Trinny Woodall's entrepreneurial spirit led her to explore various business ventures beyond television. In addition to her television appearances, she ventured into the world of beauty and fashion entrepreneurship. Notably, Woodall co-founded the beauty brand Trinny London in 2017. The brand, focused on personalized beauty solutions, gained attention for its innovative approach to makeup and skincare.

Trinny Woodall's personal life has seen its share of challenges. Her marriage to entrepreneur and former drummer Jonathan Elichaoff ended in divorce in 2009, leading to legal complexities and financial challenges. The tragic death of her ex-husband, Johnny Elichaoff, in 2014 added an emotional layer to her journey.

Despite facing personal hardships, Woodall demonstrated resilience and strength. Her ability to navigate through difficult times, both personally and professionally, showcased her determination and unwavering commitment to her craft.

Trinny Woodall's experiences as a mother have also played a significant role in shaping her perspective. Raising her daughter, Lyla Elichaoff, following the tragic loss of Lyla's father, Johnny, has added a profound dimension to Woodall's life. Her openness about the challenges of single motherhood and her close relationship with Lyla resonates with many who admire her candor and authenticity.

Trinny Woodall's journey has been marked by evolution and adaptability. From her early days in marketing to her television stardom and later ventures into entrepreneurship, she has consistently embraced change and innovation. Her transition from a fashion expert on television to a beauty entrepreneur underscores her ability to stay relevant in an ever-evolving industry.

In 2017, Trinny Woodall embarked on a new chapter in her career with the launch of Trinny London. This beauty brand is celebrated for its unique approach to makeup and skincare, focusing on personalized solutions tailored to individual needs. Trinny London's success, valued at an estimated £180 million, reflects Woodall's acumen in identifying and addressing gaps in the beauty market.

Trinny Woodall's influence extends beyond traditional television to social media platforms. Her presence on various channels, including Instagram and YouTube, allows her to connect directly with her audience. Through these platforms, she shares beauty tips, fashion insights, and snippets of her daily life, maintaining a dynamic and engaging relationship with her followers.

While Trinny Woodall has experienced success in her career and entrepreneurship, her personal life, particularly her relationships, has not been without challenges. The end of her 10-year relationship with Charles Saatchi, a noted advertising tycoon, brought forth a period of transition and self-reflection. Woodall's public acknowledgment of the breakup showcased her authenticity and willingness to share both triumphs and tribulations.

Despite facing personal and professional challenges, Trinny Woodall remains a symbol of resilience and personal growth. Her ability to navigate the complexities of life, adapt to changing circumstances, and reinvent herself demonstrates a tenacity that has garnered admiration from her audience.

Trinny Woodall's journey from a young woman navigating the world of marketing to becoming a fashion guru, media personality, and successful beauty entrepreneur is a testament to her versatility and determination. The challenges she has faced, both in her personal life and career, have not only shaped her as an individual but have also endeared her to a diverse and loyal audience.

Her impact extends beyond fashion advice; Trinny Woodall's authenticity, openness about personal struggles, and commitment to empowering individuals through beauty and style have left an indelible mark on the industry. As she continues to evolve and explore new horizons, Trinny Woodall's influence remains a dynamic force, inspiring many to embrace their unique style and face life's challenges with resilience and grace.

How She Started Her Business- Trinny London

Trinny Woodall started her beauty business, Trinny London, in 2017, after experiencing a business failure at the height of the dotcom boom. She had launched a fashion advice website called Ready2shop.com in 2000, but it went bust after 18 months, leaving her with a lot of debt and depression.

She decided to reinvent herself and pursue her passion for beauty, which she had developed since she was a teenager. She wanted to create a personalised makeup brand that would suit different skin tones, ages, and lifestyles. She also wanted to simplify the makeup process and make it more convenient and fun.

She spent four years researching, developing, and testing her products, which are based on a unique concept of stackable pots that contain cream-based formulas. She also created a digital tool called Match2Me, which helps customers find their perfect shades and products based on their skin, hair, and eye colour.

She launched Trinny London in October 2017, with an online platform and a pop-up store in London. Since then, her brand has grown rapidly, reaching customers in over 65 countries and generating millions of pounds in revenue. She has also expanded her product range, adding skincare, haircare, and fragrance products.

Trinny Woodall's business story is an inspiring example of resilience, innovation, and passion. She has used her expertise and experience in fashion and beauty to create a successful and unique brand that empowers women to feel their best.

Chapter 5: How She Became A Drug Addict and How she overcame her addiction

Trinny Woodall has chosen to openly discuss, in intricate detail, the profound impact that alcohol and drugs have had on her life and the lives of those around her. The revelations come as she prepares to inaugurate the newly relocated Hope House, a distinctive women-only rehabilitation center in London. In this candid conversation, she sheds light on the challenges of achieving sobriety, a journey she asserts was even more arduous than her recent marriage dissolution and setbacks in her television career.

The past year has presented formidable challenges for the 45-year-old TV presenter. The dissolution of her nine-year marriage to Johnny Elichaoff and her departure from ITV, where she had ruled the airwaves alongside her close friend Susannah Constantine for eight years, marked significant personal and professional upheavals. Reflecting on this tumultuous period, Woodall acknowledges the difficulties of navigating personal challenges but also recognizes the cathartic aspects of the experience.

Born Sarah-Jane Woodall, Trinny's relationship with substances began during her teenage years at a London day school, having moved from boarding school at the age of 16. The newfound freedom proved overwhelming for the shy teenager struggling with acne, leading to the initiation of drug use. By the age of 21, Trinny found herself in rehab, a challenging experience that ended abruptly after a month due to an ill-advised prank.

Despite attending Alcoholics Anonymous (AA) and Narcotics Anonymous (NA) meetings upon her return to London, Woodall struggled to commit to sobriety.

Loneliness and the allure of familiarity led her back to her old habits of drinking and drug use. She recalls an encounter in a meeting where someone suggested she hadn't hit rock bottom yet and needed a more profound experience. Trinny continued her destructive lifestyle for another five years.

The turning point came during a two-day binge with close friends, including her best friend Katy. Following this binge, the group made a pact to get sober. Trinny had made similar agreements before, but this time, something shifted. Emotionally bankrupt and feeling a void in her life, she reached out to her counselor, who arranged for her admission to a treatment center.

The journey to sobriety was not without its challenges. Trinny vividly remembers crashing her car on the way to the rehab center, swallowing tranquilizers. However, upon arrival, she experienced a profound sense of relief. Over the next two years, she hit rock bottom, spending months in rehabilitation, but ultimately surviving.

The narrative takes a poignant turn as Trinny reveals the fates of her three friends from the pact. While she managed to overcome her struggles and maintain sobriety, her best friend Katy, despite achieving sobriety, succumbed to HIV-related pneumonia. The other two friends tragically lost their lives to accidental overdoses, with one passing away while working as a journalist in Peshawar.

Trinny Woodall's journey through addiction, recovery, and the profound loss of friends underscores the complexities of battling substance abuse. Her decision to share these deeply personal experiences aims to bring awareness to the challenges of addiction and the importance of seeking help. As she inaugurates the Hope House, her openness serves as an inspiration for others struggling with similar issues, emphasizing that recovery is possible, even in the face of seemingly insurmountable obstacles.

"There were moments during my time in rehab and the halfway house that were incredibly challenging, but I never once contemplated leaving. It felt like my last opportunity, a chance to break free from the cycle of drinking and substance abuse that had consumed me," reflects Woodall thoughtfully. She recently marked 19 years of sobriety, a significant milestone in her ongoing journey.

While Woodall chooses not to delve into the specifics of her past drug use, she acknowledges having experimented with various substances, though she never resorted to injecting, eliminating concerns about HIV. The roots of her drug and alcohol use, she believes, were intricately tied to her struggles with low self-worth.

Determining the exact reasons for her choices remains a complex task. Woodall points to a familial history of alcoholism, with her grandfather and uncle grappling with the same addiction. The interplay of her upbringing, insecurities, and inherent personality likely contributed to her descent into addiction. Once ensnared in the clutches of substance abuse, she contends, the specific substance becomes somewhat inconsequential.

Following a year in rehab, Woodall transitioned to living with her parents, dedicating herself to daily Alcoholics Anonymous (AA) and Narcotics Anonymous (NA) meetings as she sought to rebuild her life without the influence of former friends. A series of secretarial and public relations jobs followed before fate intervened at a party where she met Susannah Constantine. The void left by addiction found solace in work—be it a fashion column, an unsuccessful book, a daytime TV shopping show, or an unsuccessful internet fashion business.

Their breakthrough moment came in 2001 during a makeover segment on This Morning with Richard and Judy. Despite her busy life, Woodall dismisses the notion of being a workaholic, preferring to see herself as focused, adept at multitasking, and driven by a clear sense of responsibility to her family. She rejects the negative connotations associated with "workaholic" and highlights her commitment to providing for her family, drawing parallels to a single-parent dynamic that necessitates her dedication to various responsibilities.

This week, Woodall is set to relaunch a center that originally opened its doors two decades ago. The facility, now housed in larger premises due to increased demand, is run by the charity Action on Addiction. It aims to provide second-stage, abstinence-based treatment for up to 23 women dealing with issues such as abuse, self-harm, and low self-esteem. Woodall's involvement reflects not only her personal journey but also her commitment to supporting others facing similar challenges. Her ongoing dedication to recovery, work, and making a positive impact underscores the resilience and strength she has cultivated over the years.

Trinny Woodall disclosed a poignant chapter of her past, recounting a time in her 20s when she resorted to selling all her belongings to finance a stay in a rehabilitation center. During an appearance on Steven Bartlett's Diary Of A CEO podcast, the now 59-year-old TV stylist, who boasts 30 years of sobriety, reflected on her early attempts to address her drug addiction.

Woodall described her initial experience in a residential treatment program, highlighting its confrontational nature. Unfortunately, her stay ended prematurely when she was caught watching explicit content with fellow patients. Speaking about the unorthodox methods employed in the program, she mentioned a scenario where "20 people critique how bad your life had been."

Recalling a pivotal moment in her journey to sobriety, Woodall shared the story of making a pact with three close friends to go to rehab. Acting on a rare moment of determination, she contacted a therapist, expressing the urgency of her decision. Within hours, she found herself admitted to a rehabilitation facility, financing her stay by selling her possessions. Despite facing "very tragic things" during this period, including the loss of someone she knew, Woodall persevered.

Following rehab, she spent seven months in a halfway house in Weston-super-Mare, living on a meager budget of £8 to £10 per week, covering essentials like cigarettes while working in an old people's home. Returning to London, she emerged as a profoundly transformed individual. However, the following years brought more sorrow as friends she had made the pact with succumbed to the challenges of life.

In the same interview, Woodall opened up about the tragic suicide of her ex-husband, Johnny Elichaoff, in November 2014. Despite their divorce, the two remained close, regularly communicating even after their split. Trinny, who had been shielded from the full impact of Johnny's death due to her responsibilities as a mother, only confronted the profound grief six months ago when her daughter, Lyla, left home, leaving her to grapple with the stark reality of Johnny's absence. This revelation provides a poignant glimpse into Trinny Woodall's tumultuous journey, marked by resilience, loss, and ultimately, redemption.

Chapter 6: How Trinny Woodall Built Her $250 Million Beauty Empire In Just Four Years

After an enriching virtual conversation with Trinny Woodall, it's truly astonishing that she didn't venture into the beauty business sooner. This sentiment arises not only from the meteoric success of her brand, Trinny London, standing as one of Europe's fastest-growing direct-to-consumer startups with a valuation of £180 million ($250 million), but also from the unparalleled passion she exhibits when discussing the industry—a passion that surpasses that of anyone I've ever interviewed.

Primarily recognized as the more towering half of the internationally renowned style duo Trinny and Susannah, Woodall dedicated a substantial portion of her 30s to globe-trotting. During this period, she introduced 'super slimming' style makeovers to Oprah's viewers and co-hosted television shows aimed at educating women on fashion. The most iconic among these shows is "What Not To Wear," which commemorates its 20th anniversary this year.

This breakout BBC show, stemming from their similarly named newspaper column, embarked on transformative journeys with 'fashion-challenged individuals'—individuals secretly nominated by friends and family. Trinny and Susannah's critique-filled makeover process, often teetering on the edge of offense, resonated globally, captivating audiences far and wide.

Reflecting on her past approach to styling women, Woodall acknowledges an evolution in her language. While the shows were initially rule-driven, her current communication style is much more heartfelt and relatable. From the confines of her walk-in wardrobe during our Zoom conversation, she conveys a more empathetic tone, steering away from the rigidity of past rules like "you can't wear a polo neck if you have big tits."

Woodall's involvement in "What Not To Wear" and subsequent shows across Europe, where she spent three years visiting 16 countries, solidified her understanding that the emotive feelings people have about fashion transcend factors like religion, skin color, or geographical location.

The genesis of Trinny London traces back to Woodall's contemplation of its concepts years before its official launch in 2017. As the quintessential entrepreneur, she grappled with the challenge of transitioning her ideas from mental concepts to tangible realities. This journey unfolded against the backdrop of her recognition that her personal experiences with the beauty industry presented challenges warranting thoughtful solutions for women at large.

"When I've transformed a woman, or she has participated in one of our shows, the initial thing she observes is her makeup," she expresses. "A woman's makeover isn't just about clothing; it encompasses everything. It involves her hair, makeup, new skincare routine, and sometimes her clothing—how she perceives herself as a culmination of all these elements.

"Depending on a woman's feelings about her body, she might pay more attention to her hair and makeup. It's an incredibly transformative experience. Having struggled with acne for many years, I became fixated on makeup—I wore too much, chose shades that were too orange, experimented with dreadful pink lips, every mistake in the book. I was particularly intrigued by women who weren't hiding behind layers of makeup."

Woodall began using cocaine during her teenage years, hoping it would provide the confidence that her ongoing battle with chronic acne had taken away. Over a decade and numerous visits to rehab were necessary for her recovery from addiction.

"The most significant change for me at 50, said in the most polite way possible, was that I no longer cared much about what people thought. This allowed me to be true to myself, my ideals, and pursue what I wanted to do."

Serendipitously, this marked the inception of Trinny London.

After months of crafting the brand's initial 50 SKUs at her kitchen table, Woodall hosted full Trinny London makeovers for 200 women in her bathroom.

"It was a very hands-on approach to developing the algorithm we now have," she explains. The brand was always designed to be digital-first, relying on advanced algorithms. "It needed to start with emotion, not with a group of tech experts devising a clever strategy. It had to begin with emotion and then be translated by tech experts with a clever strategy."

The women who would ultimately be drawn in by these algorithms, hopefully becoming customers, were at the core of every idea Woodall conceptualized.

"When I first pitched to Unilever for funding, Olivier [Garel], the lead of Unilever Ventures, asked, 'Who's your target market?' I responded, 'It's more about attitude than age.' I don't believe people should be categorized solely by age. When I see brands selling menopausal creams—as a menopausal woman—it's the last thing I want to buy.

"There are many women aged 50 to 60 who grew up in an era where everything in beauty was heavily retouched, and the terms used were 'anti-ageing,' 'youth-making,' you know? I want to—" she jokingly pretends to vomit "—over these words. They're so patronizing.

"I don't think we should all follow the same path in life. I've been using Botox since I was 35. Everyone should be able to choose their own path with the tools they prefer."

Hence, Woodall aimed for Trinny London's website to be as inclusive as possible, allowing every customer the opportunity to see someone resembling them wearing a product they're interested in. Presently, the lookbook features 120 non-professional models.

"Purchasing is about trust," she asserts. "Building that trust is something I likely learned in the 2000s because, when filming, you have to quickly get to know someone—to establish intimacy, to discover what truly makes them tick—even if you've only met them two minutes before."

Woodall attributes the success of Trinny London to the myriad lessons learned throughout the '90s and early '00s, including the poignant failure of her initial business venture.

"I started my career trading commodities," she remarks. "Thinking I should conform to that image—being the youngest of six kids, my dad was a banker—I soon realized I detested it."

Seeking something new, she sensed that the nascent stages of the dot-com boom presented unparalleled opportunities. "In '99, I raised funds for an online business, securing £7 million [$9.6 million] in three months. Achieving pitch to closure in that timeframe is unheard of now."

"I got a taste of that, and then the dot-com bubble burst, and we couldn't really demonstrate how we were going to be profitable. I learned a lot from that."

When it was time to secure funding for Trinny London, Woodall was determined to raise only what the business genuinely needed to launch, and she committed to growing her teams slowly.

"You can build a team too quickly, filling it with many qualified people, because you might not feel knowledgeable in the space. I remember paying the CMO £100,000 [$138,500]—this was in 1999—and she didn't deliver at all.

"I had a COO from a bank because I wasn't sure if I understood how to run a business. By the time I got to this ripe age, starting this business, I think I had learned enough in different sectors. I managed the financial side of Susannah and my business, including negotiations and contracts. So, I'm very comfortable with that.

"You bring everything you know when you start, then look for the smartest people you can hire—at the right time—to help you grow to the next stage."

For the first year and a half, Trinny London had only Woodall, COO Mark McGuinness-Smith, and a few interns on staff. Today, there are over 120 employees.

"I've had the most aggressive growth plan compared to my COO and CMO, and we've still outperformed all of our projections every year since we launched," she says.

By 2019, returning customers were the main drivers of sales, and Trinny London was growing at a rate of 350% year-on-year.

"A lot of investors say you need to have 70% new customers, 30% existing customers, but Mark and I wanted to build this business with big bricks, not quicksand.

"I've never been interested in that really high churn for high growth, but that was difficult when we did our second raise because some companies wanted to see that Glossier trajectory, and they didn't mind the high churn. But we said no. We want that lifetime value customer; she's a huge chatter, she talks to other women, she's talking now to the mainstream woman, and she was the early adopter. And that really grows the business.

"We're going to do £45 million ($62 million) this financial year."

Against all odds, the company has not only survived but thrived throughout the coronavirus pandemic.

"That first week in March, we were thinking, 'it's so inappropriate to be advertising,' so we cut all advertisement. We were feeling that shock and paralysis that was everywhere," Woodall admits. "Then we noticed that, organically, we were super high in our sales a week later."

On a whim, they turned all Facebook ads back on, unchanged, and spent the next month setting up technology that would enable them to host virtual appointments with potential customers.

"We were one of the first ones to do it, and 3000 went in a day," she says. "We realized that this collection of women, who may have been a follower but not a customer, were sitting at home wanting to try something new. And because we're not heavy, heavy makeup, it's about education, and buying something that makes you feel good."

Trinny London has grown another 280% from March 2020 through January 2021, delivering £37.7 million ($52.1 million) in gross revenue over the last 12 months.

With a full, camera-ready smile, Woodall notices I have a wall of Post-Its behind me. She walks her laptop over to a Post-It of her own. Perfectly color-coordinated, each marks a significant moment in the business's growth, as well as upcoming releases.

"It's immediate. I can see, this January, we've done 4.7, so I look at that, I see the growth, then it's easy to see what things take us to the next stage; a change in tech, an A-star launch. I look at August and know it might be a hundred-grand spike."

Previous 'A-star launches', like tinted serum-skincare hybrid BFF DeStress, have not only pushed the business's baseline up by £50k ($69k) in a day but resulted in long-term boosts. Trinny London now sells one BFF product every 70 seconds.

"There isn't actually anything on the market that compares to it," she says. "I want DeStress to have the share of the market that DoubleWear has. That's how big I think it can be."

But she won't stop there. This year, Woodall plans to release three 'gold star' launches ("a hugely innovative new product or category"), two 'silver star' launches ("a set in an existing category"), and four shade extensions.

More that Followed

Trinny Woodall, renowned for her fashion makeovers, embarked on a new venture in 2017 with the establishment of her premium makeup brand, Trinny London. Today, her brand is rapidly emerging as one of the fastest-growing direct-to-consumer (D2C) entities, propelled by a range of cream-based, skincare/makeup hybrids, an intuitive online personalization tool, and a flourishing global community.

Woodall, with a rich history cohosting makeover shows like "What Not to Wear" and "Trinny and Susannah Undress," recognized a crucial gap in the makeup industry during her extensive career. Drawing on insights gained from makeover sessions with over 3,000 women, she identified the overwhelming challenge women faced at traditional makeup counters due to the sheer array of choices. This realization became the catalyst for Trinny London.

At the helm as CEO, Woodall's brand introduced Match2Me technology, a personalized algorithm delivering makeup recommendations tailored to individual combinations of skin, hair, and eye color. The brand's emphasis on color synergy and the interplay between different makeup elements has resonated well, with 75 percent of sales flowing through the Match2Me platform.

Trinny London's origin story involves a meticulous three-year development period, during which Woodall decided that the brand's distinctiveness deserved a dedicated online space. Jane Henderson, Global President of Beauty and Personal Care at Mintel, became the brand's first investor, captivated by the concept of portability, ease, cream-based products, personalization, and community. Additional investors, including Unilever, soon joined the fold.

The brand's growth has been substantial, with a three to fourfold increase in revenue each year since its inception. In 2020, Trinny London achieved a turnover of £45 million ($62 million), marking a significant upswing from the previous year. Customer loyalty plays a pivotal role, with 80 percent of the brand's inaugural 2017 customers continuing to make purchases. Trinny London's global outreach includes shipping to 157 countries, and its customer distribution organically evolved to approximately 55 percent in the U.K., 16 percent in Australia, 11 percent in the U.S., and the remainder worldwide.

Trinny London stands out for its stackable, multitasking products presented in cream formulations, epitomized by cult favorites like BFF Cream and BFF De-Stress. These products offer both coverage and skincare benefits, aligning with Woodall's dedication to active ingredients and transparency. The brand's commitment to authenticity extends to its content-heavy approach, leveraging social media to foster an emotive relationship with its target audience.

The Trinny Tribe, comprising around 28,300 members, amplifies the brand's message globally. Trinny London's uniqueness lies in transcending the traditional makeup brand identity, resonating with its audience as a feeling, a way of life, and an ethos to embrace. Woodall's vision for beauty centers on feeling full of life, invigorated, and ready for anything, encapsulating the essence of Trinny London's mission as it continues to grow and diversify its product offerings in the coming years.

How She Faced Skepticism
Trinny Woodall faced initial skepticism when she launched her skincare and makeup company, Trinny London, in 2017. However, she successfully transformed it into a thriving business, experiencing a surge in sales during the COVID-19 pandemic.

Trinny London offers a diverse range of makeup shades, colors, and coverage options, along with skincare tailored to specific skin types and concerns. A user-friendly online tool aids customers in selecting products that complement their needs and support their skin.

Woodall attributes part of the brand's success during the pandemic to its online nature, stating that the business tripled or quadrupled its growth. She notes that this period marked a turning point for the beauty industry, where brands relying heavily on in-person sales faced challenges transitioning to an online-centric model.

Beyond the product itself, Woodall emphasizes the importance of reaching the right audience. She believes that building a modern business in her industry involves creating a community of women and communicating with them effectively. Social media has played a pivotal role in achieving this, with Woodall leveraging her personal and Trinny London's accounts, along with online community groups known as "Trinny Tribes."

Being genuine and realistic online is a central element of Trinny London's brand strategy. Woodall emphasizes the need for authenticity, presenting products in an unfiltered and accessible way. The brand aims to strike a balance between realism and aspiration, tailoring its message to resonate with customers rather than relying on conventional marketing approaches.

Securing investment has been a crucial aspect of Trinny London's growth. Despite facing challenges in marketing a female-focused brand to predominantly male venture capitalists, Woodall succeeded in raising funds. She encountered resistance and skepticism, with some VCs seeking input from assistants or suggesting that older women wouldn't buy from an online-focused brand. Nevertheless, Trinny London's valuation reached $250 million in early

2021, and it generated £59.8 million ($74 million) in revenue in 2021.

Woodall acknowledges the importance of storytelling for female founders, emphasizing the need to articulate the vision clearly. Her advice to fellow female founders centers on staying focused on their ideas and goals, avoiding distractions by not overly comparing themselves to others. Woodall encourages maintaining belief in one's vision and persevering with dedication.

Printed in Great Britain
by Amazon